Just Joking 7

NATIONAL
GEOGRAPHIC
KiDS

Just Joking 7

7

300
hilarious jokes
about everything,
including tongue
twisters, riddles,
and more!

Rosie Gowsell Pattison

NATIONAL GEOGRAPHIC
WASHINGTON, D.C.

KNOCK,
KNOCK.
Who's there?
Feline.
Feline who?
I had a feline you'd be home.

What eats nuts and solves mysteries?

Q

A

Squirrel-lock Holmes.

Say this fast three times:

Louise sneezes when she sees cheeses.

Q What do you call the horse next door?

A Your neigh-bor.

DOG 1:
Can we paws awhile? We've been running for ages.

DOG 2:
Good idea. I'm really fur-sty.

6

KNOCK, KNOCK.

Who's there?
Thermos.
Thermos who?
Thermos be a better way to talk to you.

A chameleon's tongue can shoot out of its mouth at 13 miles an hour (21 km/h)!

KNOCK, KNOCK.

Who's there?
Fish.
Fish who?
Gesundheit!

There are about 120 species of pufferfish. The smallest species is only one inch (2.5 cm) long while the largest can be up to three feet (0.9 m) long.

Q What kind of bird isn't welcome in banks?

A A robin.

SWORDFISH 1:
Wow! Your new hat is looking sharp!

SWORDFISH 2:
Thanks, it makes me feel so-fish-ticated.

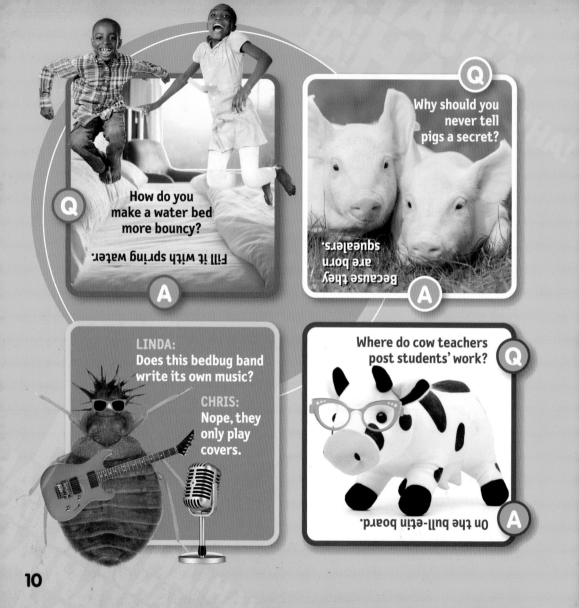

Q How do you make a water bed more bouncy?

A Fill it with spring water.

Q Why should you never tell pigs a secret?

A Because they are born squealers.

LINDA: Does this bedbug band write its own music?

CHRIS: Nope, they only play covers.

Q Where do cow teachers post students' work?

A On the bull-etin board.

KNOCK, KNOCK.

Who's there?
A plate.
A plate who?
You're a plate,
it's time to go
to bed!

Black bear cubs weigh only
a half to one pound (0.2 to
0.5 kg) at birth. That's about
the same as three apples!

KNOCK,
KNOCK.

Who's there?
You know.
You know who?
I know who,
but do you?

A blue and yellow macaw's face will blush pink when it's excited.

12

Q

What do you call a dog writing a ticket?

A

Barking enforcement.

IDRIS: I think my fruit was stolen!

LINA: Are you berry sure you left it there?

IDRIS: It just disa-pear-ed. Can you believe it?

LINA: I'm s-peach-less.

Q

What kind of pickles should you eat in spring?

A

Daffo-dills.

Q

What do mountains wear on their heads?

A

Snowcaps.

13

ANIMAL ANTICS

NAME
Skipper

FAVORITE TYPE OF BOOK
Ferry-tales

PET PEEVE
People who barge in

FAVORITE TYPE OF BOAT
Pug-boat

15

A monster's shopping list:

- Spareribs
- Scream cheese
- Fettuccine afraid-o
- Grave-y
- Deviled eggs

Q

What type of **magazines** do **COWS** like to look through?

Cattle-logs.

A

Q

What is a wolf's favorite time of year?

The howl-idays!

A

Q

What do you get if you cross a chicken with a cement mixer?

A bricklayer.

A

Where do the smartest parrots live?

Q

In the brainforest.

A

17

Q

What kind of **appetizer** should you eat in **spring?**

A A bloomin' onion.

FISH 1: Did the ocean give you detailed directions?

FISH 2: Yes, it was very Pacific.

Q

What has a ton of ears but can't hear anything?

A A corn-field.

Q

How do you make a **milkshake?**

A Give it a good scare!

Zebras have some serious fighting skills. They use strong bites and powerful kicks to fight off predators.

KNOCK, KNOCK.

Who's there?
Gift.
Gift who?
Gift me a hand with all these bags out here!

KNOCK, KNOCK.

Who's there?
Bed.
Bed who?
Bed you can't guess
who this is!

20

Tiger fossils that have been found in China are believed to be two million years old.

Q What do you call a vampire with a terrible cough?

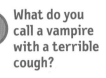

A Count Hack-ula.

COFFIN
MEDICINE

CAT 1: Look at this birthday cake!

CAT 2: Wow! Did you make this yourself?

CAT 1: Yes, I made it from scratch.

HAPPY BIRTHDAY

21

A hammerhead shark's favorite snack is a stingray. When hunting, the shark uses its long, wide head to pin the ray to the ocean floor and trap it.

KNOCK, KNOCK.

Who's there?
Raisin.
Raisin who?
Raisin shine! It's time to get up.

Say this fast three times:

Two flute tooters tutor two tooters to toot.

Q Why did the girl put sugar on her pillows?

A So she could have sweet dreams.

Q What's woolly, lives on a farm, and drinks blood?

A Count Dracu-baaaa.

Q Why did the police bring a duck to a crime scene?

A Because it is good at quacking a case.

24

25

KNOCK,
KNOCK.

Who's there?
Quack.
Quack who?
Quack open this
door and see for
yourself!

26

Famous dogs:

- Billie Ei-leash
- Dolly Paw-ton
- Droolius Caesar
- Kim Kar-dachshund
- Meghan Barkle

Q Where do amphibians watch movies?

A On Newt-flix.

Q Where do **rabbits** go for **pancakes?**

A I-HOP.

28

NAME **Harley**

FAVORITE SCHOOL SUBJECT
Cycle-ology

FAVORITE FOOD
Chimps and dip

PET PEEVE
Losing my mon-keys

Q

Why wouldn't the **balloon** listen to the **radio?**

A

Because it was scared of pop music.

Q

Why are cats terrible storytellers?

A

Because they only have one tail.

Q

Why are penguins fun at parties?

A

Because they really know how to break the ice.

SPIDER 1:
I need to unwind. I'm going on vacation.

SPIDER 2:
What are your plans?

SPIDER 1:
I'm going fly-fishing.

Sheep have an excellent sense of smell. They even have scent glands on their feet!

KNOCK, KNOCK.

Who's there?
Needle.
Needle who?
Needle little help with this lock.

Q What kind of **nut** has no **shell?**

A A doughnut.

Q What is yellow and scary?

A A boo-nana.

Q Why do people put candles on top of a birthday cake?

A Because it's too hard to put them on the bottom.

MARIE: I've started a gardening business.

FRASER: Are you making lots of money?

MARIE: I'm raking it in!

KNOCK, KNOCK.

Who's there?
Amarillo.
Amarillo who?
Amarillo nice person.

Horses have 10 different muscles in their ears and can turn them 180 degrees. The human ear only has three muscles.

KNOCK, KNOCK.

Who's there?
Harley.
Harley who?
These jokes are
Harley-rious!

An ostrich can kick
with enough force
to kill a predator
such as a lion
or hyena.

Stores at the Wacky Shopping Mall:

- **SEW WHAT?** We'll hem your pants, but we really don't care.
- **HAIR-ANOIA:** Yes, I got a haircut. Why are you asking? Is someone talking about me?
- **ABRA-KEBAB-RA:** These kebabs taste magical!
- **BEAUTY AND THE BEACH:** Oceanside makeup service.
- **PLANET OF THE GRAPES:** A world of fruits!

ELLEN: Did you like the chicken fingers?

PETRICE: No, they tasted fowl.

Q What do you call a tired vegetable?

A Slee-pea.

Q What language do billboards speak?

A Sign language.

Q Why did the farmer put oil on the mouse?

A Because it was squeaking.

Q What do you call a wild dog that uses bad language?

A A swear-wolf.

38

KNOCK, KNOCK.

Who's there?
Candice.
Candice who?
Candice be the right address?

Komodo dragons have poisonous saliva. They will sometimes bite their prey and then follow it for miles until it dies—then eat its body.

FISHERMAN 1: Should I play some music while we are fishing?

FISHERMAN 2: Yes, put on something catchy.

Q How can you tell when a flamingo is blushing?

A You can't.

Q What do you get if you cross a hawk and a piece of cheese?

A A curd of prey.

Q What kind of **movies** do **cats** like?

A Mew-sicals.

Scary ice-cream flavors:

- **Vampire Vein-illa**
- **Lemon Slime**
- **Leeches and Scream**
- **Booberry**

A polar bear's sense of smell is so strong, it can sniff out its dinner from up to nine miles (14.5 km) away!

Q What do you call a sleeping fruit?

A A nap-ricot.

TONGUE TWISTER!

Say this fast three times:

Which Swiss wristwatch will Chris miss?

Q What does a gingerbread man put on his bed?

A Cookie sheets.

Q Which bear laughs the most?

A The pand-HA!

44

Red foxes have excellent hearing. When hunting, they can hear a rodent digging underground!

KNOCK, KNOCK.

Who's there?
Icy.
Icy who?
Icy you peeking out the window!

NAME **Scribbles**

FAVORITE PASTIME
Drawing

DREAM JOB
Writer

FAVORITE QUOTE
"Lookin' sharp!"

47

GABRIEL: Hey, you have a beard now! I thought you didn't like facial hair?

BRAD: It grew on me.

Q Why do bananas whisper?

A So they don't wake up the rest of the bunch.

Q Why did the doughnut go to the dentist?

A Because it needed a chocolate filling.

Q Where do ghosts go miniature golfing?

A On a golf corpse.

Moose are huge. An adult male moose can weigh up to 1,300 pounds (600 kg). Their antlers can grow to be six feet (1.8 m) wide from tip to tip.

KNOCK, KNOCK.

Who's there?
Otto.
Otto who?
You Otto know.
Who are you?!

Q

Where do hamburgers take their dates?

To the meatball.

A

THERE'S NOTHING BETTER THAN LION AROUND AFTER A GOOD MEAL.

Q When do chickens go to bed?

A Half past hen.

Q What **letters** are **not** in the **alphabet?**

The ones in the mail.

A

Q Why couldn't **Monday** pick up a **barbell?**

A Because it's a weak-day.

Q What did the horse say when it fell over?

"Help! I can't giddyup!" **A**

54

Tapirs have long, flexible noses that they use to push things around to find food.

KNOCK, KNOCK.

Who's there?
Alfredo.
Alfredo who?
I'm too alfredo watch that scary movie.

55

KNOCK, KNOCK.

Who's there?
Gnaw.
Gnaw who?
You'll never gnaw unless you open the door.

Q Why do cats always get their way?

A They are very purr-suasive.

Q Why did the superhero flush the toilet?

A Because it was his doody!

Q What kind of tests do they take in beauty school?

A Makeup exams.

Q What is a whale's favorite kind of candy?

A Blubber gum.

57

What do you call an astronaut lamb?

A rocket sheep.

HA! HA! HA! HA!

ASHA:
Do you think I'd be faster without my shell?

ADITYA:
I think you would be more sluggish.

What do you call a raven in winter?

A brrrr-d.

KNOCK, KNOCK.

Who's there?
Tortoise.
Tortoise who?
Our teacher has tortoise well.

Red-footed tortoises can live to be 50 years old or more.

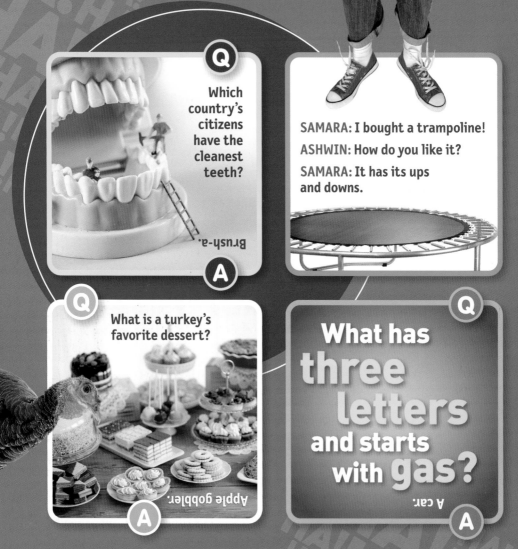

Q

Which country's citizens have the cleanest teeth?

A

Brush-a.

SAMARA: I bought a trampoline!

ASHWIN: How do you like it?

SAMARA: It has its ups and downs.

Q

What is a turkey's favorite dessert?

A

Apple gobbler.

Q

What has **three letters** and starts with **gas?**

A

A car.

62

Q What do butterflies sleep on?

A Cater-pillows.

Q What do fish use to hear better?

A Herring aids.

There are more than 20 species of macaque in more than nine countries around the world.

KNOCK, KNOCK.

Who's there?
Lime.
Lime who?
Sorry lime late!

ANIMAL ANTICS

Q What kind of car does an egg drive?

A A Volks-wagen.

Q How do dolphins make decisions?

A They flipper coin.

DEAN: Did you hear the hot dog movie won an award?

SAM: It's an Oscar wiener!

Q Where did the kittens play at the birthday party?

A In the pounce house.

70

The average American alligator can be 10 to 15 feet (3 to 5 m) long, but half of that length is its huge tail!

KNOCK, KNOCK.

Who's there?
Orange.
Orange who?
Orange you going to invite me in?

71

DINER: Will my pizza be long?

WAITER: No, it will be round.

PIZZA
PIZZA
PIZZA

Q What did the **blanket** **say** to the **bed?**

A "I've got you covered."

Q What kind of fish do you find in a birdcage?

A A perch.

FARMER 1: I heard a bunch of jokes about sheep today.

FARMER 2: You should tell them to your sheepdog!

FARMER 1: Nah, he's herd them all.

KNOCK,
KNOCK.

Who's there?
G.I.
G.I. who?
G.I. don't know.

Despite their cute appearance, Tasmanian devils are dangerous! They spin in circles, screech, and bite ferociously when attacked.

AUDIENCE MEMBER: How much does it cost to hear a roof joke?

COMEDIAN: This one is on the house.

Q How does an **ice-cream cone** travel?

A By fudge-cycle.

Q What do you call two raspberries playing guitars?

A A jam session.

Q What do you call an earthquake in a cemetery?

A A graveyard shift.

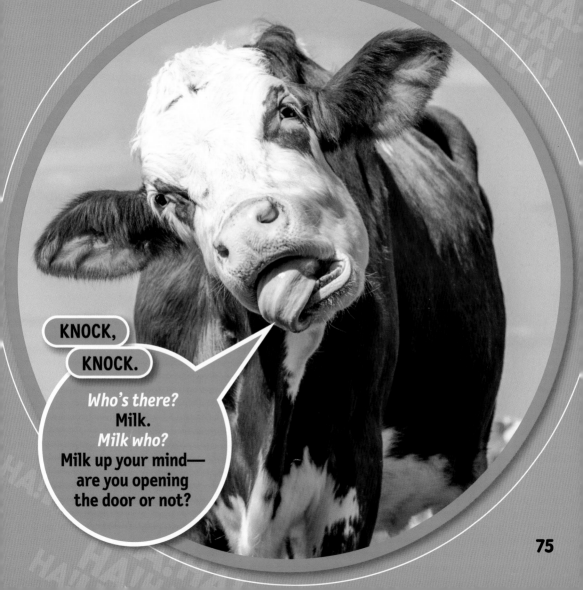

75

Q What do you get if you cross a cat and a kitchen tool?

A A whisker.

Q What kind of music do chiropractors listen to?

A Hip-pop.

Q Why do nurses need red crayons?

A So they can draw blood.

Legend has it that goats discovered coffee. A herder noticed that goats became energetic and unable to sleep after eating berries from an unfamiliar tree. The herder tried the berries, and coffee was born.

KNOCK, KNOCK.

Who's there?
Goat.
Goat who?
Here we goat again!

Q What is **big, green,** and plays lots of **tricks?**

A Prank-enstein.

GAMER 1: Did you see the new Minecraft movie?

GAMER 2: It was a blockbuster!

Q What kind of music does cheese listen to?

A R & Brie.

Q Why did the cell phone call the dentist?

A It was having trouble with its Bluetooth.

Animal princesses:

- Snow Great White
- Cinderella-phant
- Tinker-bull
- Po-cat-hontas
- Moo-lan

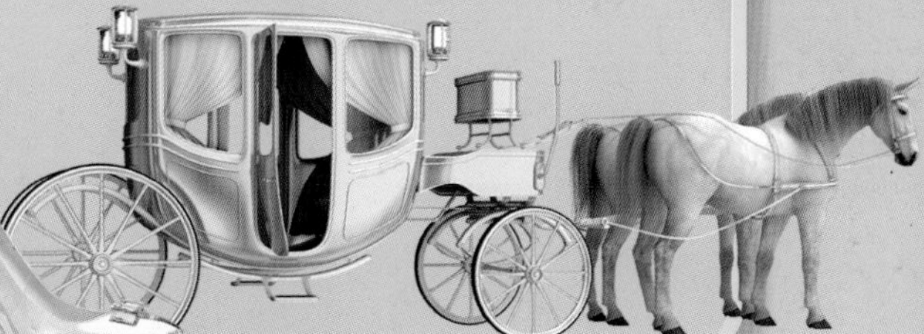

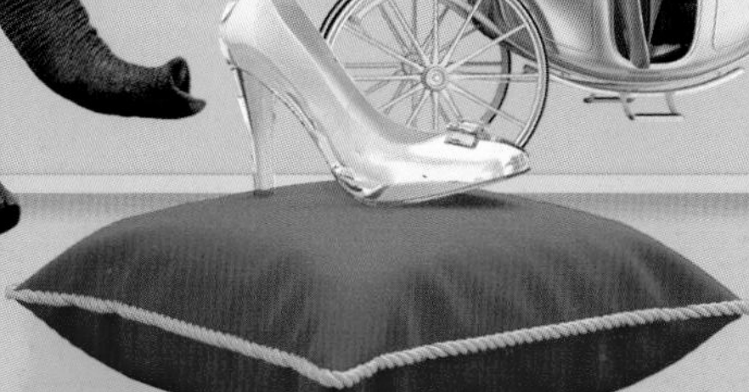

Elephants use their trunks as snorkels when in deep water. They walk on the riverbed and stick their trunks up to the surface to breathe.

KNOCK, KNOCK.

Who's there?
Savannah.
Savannah who?
I'm Savannah hard time hearing you through this door.

Q

What is a cat's favorite kind of sticker?

A Scratch and sniff.

TONGUE TWISTER!

Say this fast three times:

Lucky Luke likes lakes.

Q

How do you measure a snake?

A In inches—they don't have feet.

Q

What's **black** and **white** and swims in the **ocean?**

A A sea-bra.

Q

How do you row a **boatful** of **puppies?**

With a doggy paddle.

A

A lion's tongue is covered in sharp points called papillae. These are used to help scrape meat off of bones.

KNOCK, KNOCK.

Who's there?
Queso.
Queso who?
I've got a bad queso the sniffles.

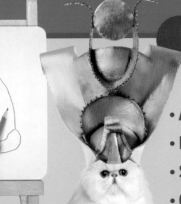

Famous cats:

- Alexander Ha-meow-lton
- Pi-cat-so
- Shakes-purr
- Cleo-cat-ra
- Michelle Oba-meow

MARCUS: Why are you putting peanut butter on my dog?

ELLE: You said it was pure bread.

ROWAN: I just opened a cheese store.

WESTON: You gotta brie kidding!

ROWAN: I thought it was a gouda business idea.

Yes, We're OPEN

Q How do you get to Dentist Island?

Take the tooth ferry.

A

Q What did the beaver say to the tree?

"Nice gnawing you."

A

Q Why did the kitten get lost?

He found the directions purr-plexing.

A

88

KNOCK, KNOCK.

Who's there?
Taco.
Taco who?
Let's taco-ver the phone instead.

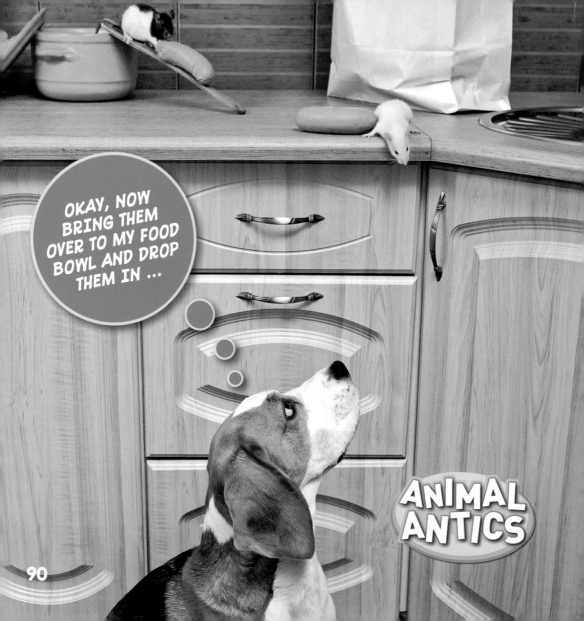

Q How do **sea birds** search the **internet?**

A They use Goo-gull.

CUSTOMER: So how has business been lately?

TAILOR: Sew-sew.

91

Animal jobs:

- Comedi-hens
- Bear-port security guard
- Baa-ber
- Hiss-tory teacher
- Bark-aeologist

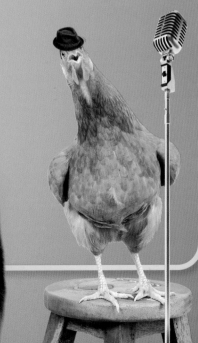

KNOCK, KNOCK.

Who's there?
Scott.
Scott who?
I've Scott to go to the bathroom! Open the door!

The Eastern glass lizard looks like a snake. It has no legs and a tail that is easily broken off. That is how it earned the name "glass."

LOUISE: Did you eat at that new pasta restaurant?

STEPHEN: About a week orzo ago.

LOUISE: I bet it cost a pretty penne.

STEPHEN: I was alfredo to look at the bill.

Q

What do you call a cute loaf of bread?

A-dough-rable.

A

Q

What do you get if you cross a potato and a baseball team?

SPUDS

The New York Yam-kees.

A

Q

What kind of **car** did the **cook** want to **drive?**

A Chef-rolet.

A

95

Say this fast three times:

Fresh fried French fries.

Q

What kind of shoes do spies wear?

Sneakers.

A

Q

Where do library books sleep?

Under their covers.

A

Q

Why is Dracula always annoying people?

Because he's a pain in the neck.

A

KNOCK, KNOCK.

Who's there?
Barley.
Barley who?
I missed my bus and barley made it here on time.

Spoonbills get their name from their large, flat, spoon-shaped bills. They use them to scoop up minnows, plants, and small crustaceans in shallow water.

ANIMAL ANTICS

Q What does a baby computer call its father?

A Data.

Q Why do **COWS** lie down in **groups** when it's **cold?**

A To keep each udder warm.

There are more than 200 species of squirrels. They live on every continent except Australia and Antarctica.

KNOCK, KNOCK.

Who's there?
Accordion.
Accordion who?
Accordion to my schedule, it's time to leave.

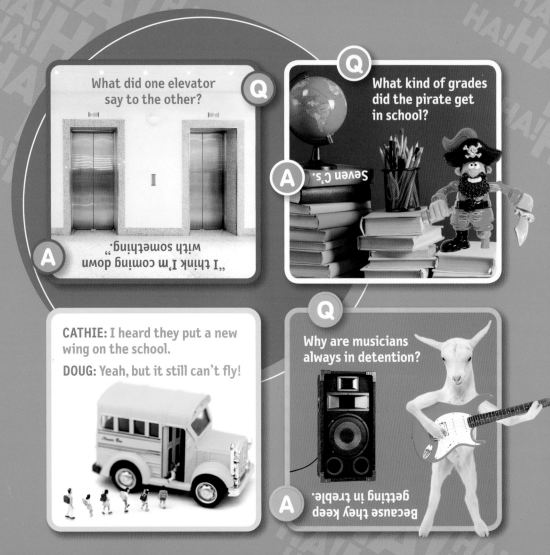

Q What did one elevator say to the other?

A "I think I'm coming down with something."

Q What kind of grades did the pirate get in school?

A Seven C's.

CATHIE: I heard they put a new wing on the school.

DOUG: Yeah, but it still can't fly!

Q Why are musicians always in detention?

A Because they keep getting in treble.

KNOCK, KNOCK.

Who's there?
Pasta.
Pasta who?
It's pasta-ble
we're lost.

What did one slice of bread say to the other on their wedding day?

"It was loaf at first sight!"

MOM: So, what's your dream job?

DAUGHTER: I think I'd like to work in a mirror factory.

MOM: Really? Why?

DAUGHTER: I don't know. I can just see myself working there.

Q Where does smart butter go?

A On honor rolls.

Q What kind of pictures do turtles take?

A Shell-fies.

Q Why was the trash can sad?

A It got dumped.

106

KNOCK,

KNOCK.

Who's there?
Farm.
Farm who?
Is your
farm-ily home?

Pigs can grow to
weigh 700 pounds
(318 kg)—or
even more!

Q What is the **best way** to **carve wood?**

A Whittle by whittle.

Q What's **round, hairy,** and wears **sunglasses?**

A A coconut on vacation.

Q

What kind of award do you give a dentist?

A A little plaque.

Say this fast three times:

Thirty-three thirsty thrushes.

Q

What does the heaviest bone weigh?

A A skele-ton.

Q

What **sound** does a **witch's cereal** make?

A Snap, cackle, and pop.

How does a mouse feel after a bath?

Q

Squeaky clean.

A

ANIMAL ANTICS

Q What do you call a snowman searching through a bunch of carrots?

A A nose picker.

Q Where do **celebrities camp?**

A The Hollywoods.

Q What do sloths like to read?

A Snooze-papers.

Q Why did the drum take a nap?

A Because it was beat.

114

Potato cods get their name from the potato-shaped markings on their backs.

KNOCK, KNOCK.

Who's there?
Cod.
Cod who?
Cod I come in?

Bird presidents:

- John F. Hen-nedy
- Theodore Rooster-velt
- Barack Owl-bama
- Crow Biden
- Martin Van Heron
- Ronald Raven

Q How do clowns like their eggs cooked?

A Funny-side up.

Hippos have the largest teeth of all land mammals. Their front teeth can grow up to 1.5 feet (46 cm) in length.

KNOCK, KNOCK.

Who's there?
Echo.
Echo who?
Who, who, who, who.

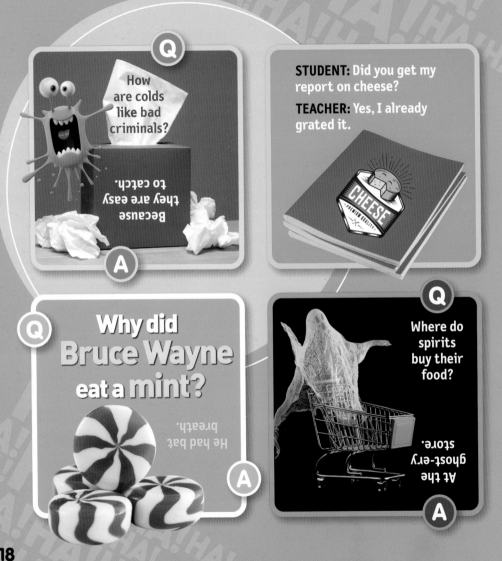

Q How are colds like bad criminals?

A Because they are easy to catch.

STUDENT: Did you get my report on cheese?

TEACHER: Yes, I already grated it.

Q **Why did Bruce Wayne eat a mint?**

A He had bat breath.

Q Where do spirits buy their food?

A At the ghost-ery store.

Great white sharks are able to swallow seals whole!

KNOCK, KNOCK.

Who's there?
Fin.
Fin who?
I can let myself fin.

Q How do monkeys get down the stairs?

A They slide down the banana-ster.

Q What has a **long neck, four legs, and flower petals?**

A A giraffe-odil.

Q What does a ghost panda eat?

A Bam-BOO!

GARY:
Did you write down all the letters of the alphabet?

JAMES:
Only 25 of them.

GARY:
How did that happen?

JAMES:
I don't know y.

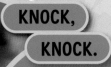

A group of foxes is called a skulk.

123

Q

What do sharks order at McDonald's?

A quarter flounder
with cheese.

KID MONSTER: This pizza is scary good!

MOM MONSTER: Slow down! Stop goblin your food.

Q How did Godzilla feel after eating too many houses?

A Homesick.

KNOCK, KNOCK.

Who's there?
Crow.
Crow who?
I'll crow away if you don't open the door.

Crows will sometimes rub ants into their feathers to help get rid of parasites. This behavior is called anting.

How to tell if there's a snowman living in your house:

- Someone has turned the air-conditioning up as high as it will go.
- All of the carrots are missing.
- There are puddles near the oven.
- You find a top hat and corncob pipe in the closet.

Q What do zombies put on their fries?

A Grave-y.

EGG 1:
I want to be a comedian. I like to crack people up.

EGG 2:
You are such a practical yolker.

KNOCK,

KNOCK.

Who's there?
Betta.
Betta who?
I betta be at the
right place
this time.

Betta fish have a special
organ called a labyrinth,
which allows them to
breathe air from the
surface of the water.

Q

How do monsters like their eggs?

Terri-fried.

A

TONGUE TWISTER!

Say this fast three times:

Six swift swans swim sweetly.

Q

What do you do if you are scared of elevators?

Take steps to avoid them.

A

Q

What did the thumb say to the finger?

"I'm in glove with you!"

A

KNOCK, KNOCK.

Who's there?
Owl.
Owl who?
I'm owl by myself out here.

An owl can turn its head 270 degrees.

HA! HA! HA!

133

ANIMAL ANTICS

NAMES
Ham-ilton and Curly

FAVORITE HAIRSTYLE
Pigtails

FAVORITE HOLIDAY
Ar-boar Day

FAVORITE MOVIE CHARACTER
Ham Solo

IT'S SNOUT WARM ENOUGH. I'M NOT SWIMMING TODAY.

Q

What is a foot's favorite snack?

A

Dori-toes.

Q

Why didn't the gardener plant an herb garden?

A

Because she couldn't find the thyme.

LEAH:
I bought a new pair of gloves today, but they are both lefties.

RUTH:
On the one hand, that's great. On the other hand, it's not.

Q

What is **big** and **gray** and puts people to **sleep?**

A

A hypno-potamus.

136

KNOCK, KNOCK.

Who's there?
Dozen.
Dozen who?
Dozen anyone ever open this door?

A group of dolphins is called a pod.

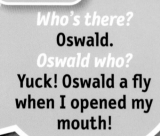

KNOCK, KNOCK.

Who's there?
Oswald.
Oswald who?
Yuck! Oswald a fly when I opened my mouth!

Icelandic horses are short and sturdy. They only grow to be around five feet (1.5 m) tall.

KID:
Do you have any books about sea turtles?

LIBRARIAN:
Hardback?

KID:
Yes, with little heads and flippers.

Animal games:

- Hide-and-Beak
- Stable Tennis
- Bat-minton
- Flam-bingo

Q What do you call a tired woodcutter?

A A slumber-jack.

Q How do chickens leave the coops?

A They use the eggs-it.

STUDENT: I'm going to study soda when I grow up.

TEACHER: That isn't a real job.

STUDENT: Yes it is—it's called a fizz-icist!

TEACHER: You should be a pop star instead.

Q Where do French fry boxers fight?

A In an onion ring.

Q

What is a kangaroo's favorite candy?

Lolli-hops.

A

141

ANIMAL
ANTICS

GRIZZLY 1: Look at the salmon I caught!

GRIZZLY 2: Wow! Did you catch that with your bear hands?

Q What is an ape's favorite snack?

A A chocolate chimp cookie.

144

The fennec fox's massive ears disperse body heat to help regulate its body temperature.

KNOCK,

KNOCK.

Who's there?
Ears.
Ears who?
Ears another knock-knock joke!

Brook trouts' speckles help camouflage them from predators like birds and otters.

146

Q

What do you call someone who eats **a lot** of **chocolate?**

A A cocoa-nut.

Q

What's green and barks?

A Broc-collie.

Q

What kind of chips do they sell at the airport?

A Plane.

Q

What do you call a **ghost chicken?**

A Poultry-geist.

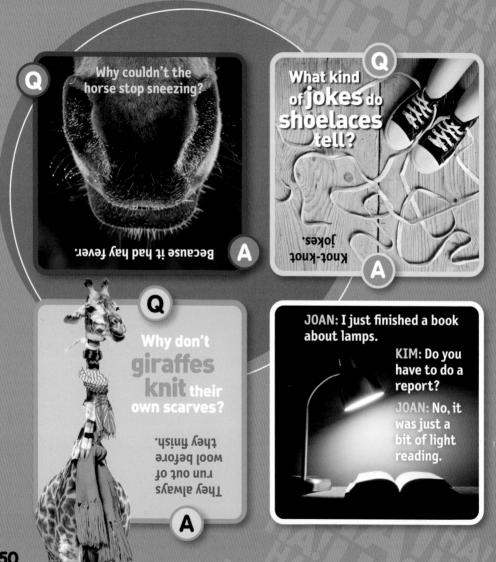

Q Why couldn't the horse stop sneezing?

A Because it had hay fever.

Q What kind of **jokes** do **shoelaces** tell?

A Knot-knot jokes.

Q Why don't **giraffes knit** their own scarves?

A They always run out of wool before they finish.

JOAN: I just finished a book about lamps.

KIM: Do you have to do a report?

JOAN: No, it was just a bit of light reading.

KNOCK, KNOCK.

Who's there?
Weirdo.
Weirdo who?
Weirdo you think you're going?

The loon appears on the Canadian one dollar coin. This coin is called the loonie.

153

Q Which reindeer has the worst manners?

A Rude-olph.

KEEP OFF THE GRASS

Q What do you call a **brain** in a **library?**

A A mind reader.

The red-eyed tree frog's flashy colors distract predators while it runs to safety.

KNOCK, KNOCK.

Who's there?
Curd.
Curd who?
I got here as fast as my legs curd carry me.

What do you find on a lizard's floor?

Q

Rep-tiles.

A

How does Mr. Claus keep his hands clean?

Q

He uses hand Santa-tizer.

A

Buffalo—including this African buffalo—and bison look alike, but they are different species. One way to tell them apart is to check for a beard: Bison have them and buffalo don't!

KNOCK, KNOCK.

Who's there?
Herd.
Herd who?
I herd you were home so I stopped by.

157

159

Q

Why are pigs bad drivers?

A

They hog the road.

Q Why did the snail cross the road?

A I don't know; he didn't get there yet.

Q What do monsters call their parents?

A Mummy and Dead-y.

Q Why should you never write a book on polar bears?

A Because writing on paper is much easier.

Q What has **two legs, pockets, and** is really **scary?**

A Boo jeans.

KNOCK, KNOCK.

Who's there?
Salmon.
Salmon who?
Will salmon please open this door?!

Hippos love nightlife! They live in very warm climates so they do most of their eating at night when it's cooler.

Q What kind of car does a snake drive?

A An ana-Honda.

Q What kind of cheese do mice put on their pizza?

A Mouse-arella.

166

KNOCK, KNOCK.

Who's there?
Waddle.
Waddle who?
Waddle we do today?

Stingrays migrate in large groups called fevers. There can be up to 10,000 stingrays in one fever!

Q

What do you call sausages that go trick-or-treating?

Hallo-wieners.

A

Q What kind of trees do pigs plant?

A Ma-hog-any.

Q What kind of **meal** is always **cold?**

A A brrrr-ger.

Q What did a *T. rex* get on its feet instead of blisters?

A Dino-sores.

FARMER 1: I have a secret to tell you but no one else can know.

FARMER 2: Shhh, not here. The potatoes have eyes and the corn have ears.

Q

What do you do with a criminal sheep?

A

Put it behind baas.

PATIENT: Doctor, I swallowed my allowance!

DOCTOR: Let's see if there's any change in the morning.

Q

What do you get if you cross a chicken and a cow?

A

Roost beef.

What do baby cats wear?

Q

A

Diapurrrs.

172

A female saltwater crocodile can lay up to 80 eggs at one time.

KNOCK, KNOCK.

Who's there?
Weekend.
Weekend who?
Weekend do anything we want!

174

Q What's **black** and **white** and **noisy?**

A A zebra playing a trumpet.

Q Who keeps track of an insect's money?

A An account-ant.

Q What has 40 legs but can't walk?

A Twenty pairs of pants.

TONGUE TWISTER!

Say this fast three times:

Sloppy Slurpees.

A newborn puppy can't poop on its own. It needs its mother's help.

KNOCK, KNOCK.

Who's there?
Figs.
Figs who?
Figs the doorbell—
I've been knocking forever.

177

What kind of dog does a snowman have?

A slush puppy.

KNOCK, KNOCK.

Who's there?
Chickens.
Chickens who?
No, chickens cluck.
Owls who.

Chickens are living descendants of *Tyrannosaurus rex*.

Q What is a violinist's favorite snack?

A String cheese.

Q What can **fly** underwater?

A A bee in a submarine.

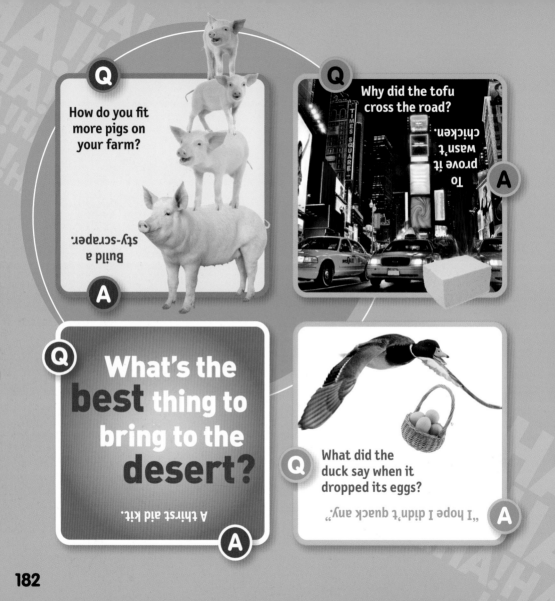

Q How do you fit more pigs on your farm?

A Build a sty-scraper.

Q Why did the tofu cross the road?

A To prove it wasn't chicken.

Q What's the **best** thing to bring to the **desert?**

A A thirst aid kit.

Q What did the duck say when it dropped its eggs?

A "I hope I didn't quack any."

Shrews move *fast!* They rarely stop moving. This means they have to eat a lot! In fact, they must eat every few hours to survive.

KNOCK, KNOCK.

Who's there?
Amy.
Amy who?
Amy 'fraid
of the dark!

Q What kind of androids do you find at the North Pole?

A Snow-bots.

Q Why did the tree get in trouble?

A It was being knotty.

184

TONGUE TWISTER!

Say this fast three times:

Gobbling gargoyles gobbled gobbling goblins.

Q Where are **totally average things made?**

A At the satisfactory.

Ring-tailed coatis are closely related to raccoons. A large group of coatis is called a band.

185

What do you call a piece of bacon that has been sunbathing all day?

Done.

A

Q What did the giraffe wear to the fancy dinner party?

A Ten bow ties.

BIRD 1:
Did you have fun at the owl's party last night?

BIRD 2:
It was a hoot!

188

KNOCK,

KNOCK.

Who's there?
Ice-cream soda.
Ice-cream soda who?
Ice-cream soda
people can
hear me.

Double-crested cormorants turn
black as they get older. They can
live to be up to 23 years old.

ANIMAL ANTICS

Q What do you get if you cross a duck with a sea monster?

A A quacken.

TEACHER: Our class trip is to a cola factory!

STUDENT: That's soda-lightful!

TEACHER: There will be a pop quiz when we get back.

Q What do cows text their friends?

A E-moo-jis.

Q What do you call an alien with three eyes?

A Aliiien.

KNOCK,

KNOCK.

Who's there?
Toothpick.
Toothpick who?
Hurry up! We have to
leave toothpick up
your grandma!

The crested black
macaque gets its name
from the tuft of hair on
the top of its head.

What is a squirrel's favorite ballet?

The Nutcracker.

Q Why did the baker quit making doughnuts?

A He was fed up with the hole business.

BUNNY 1: Why are you eating that wedding ring?

BUNNY 2: Because I heard it was 18 carrots.

Q What do you call a dog in a hammock?

A A rocker spaniel.

Q What is the creepiest kind of prehistoric creature?

A A scare-odactyl.

Antarctic fur seals are more agile on land than other seals. They can use their front flippers to sit up and walk on land.

KNOCK, KNOCK.

Who's there?
Lemon.
Lemon who?
Lemon know when you are ready to go.

What do you find in a **ghost's nose?**

Boo-gers.

SYLVIO:
Why are you tossing coins at that beluga?

FRANK:
I thought it was a wishing whale.

KNOCK, KNOCK.

Who's there?
Woo.
Woo who?
I'm glad you're so excited!

A ring-tailed lemur's tail is longer than its body. The lemur uses its tail to wave a stinky odor at its rivals.

Q What is the
Abominable
Snowman's
favorite
pasta?

A Spag-yeti.

JOKEFINDER

JOKEFINDER

204

ILLUSTRATIONCREDITS

Stockphoto Mania/SS (bottom, right); 94, Dan Rieck/DRMS; 95, Guzel Gashigullina/SS (top, left), Pixel Shot/SS (top, right), Richard Peterson/SS (top, right), Adrey_Popov/SS (bottom, left), Panda Studio/SS (bottom, left), Pixelrobot/DRMS (bottom, left), Aliakseyenka Mikita/SS (bottom, right), Mtsaride/SS (bottom, left); 96, Photobac/DRMS (top, right), Studiovin/SS (bottom, left), Yeti Studio/SS (bottom, left), Elena Khramova/DRMS (bottom, right); 97, Moose Henderson/DRMS; 98, Bachkova Natalia/SS; 100, Chernetskaya/DRMS (top), ifong/SS (top, middle), Madlen/SS (top, middle), Sally Wallis/DRMS (bottom); 101, Sue Feldberg/DRMS; 102, Pavel Losevsky/DRMS (top, left), Aboikis/SS (top, right), Peyker/SS (top, right), Grafner/DRMS (bottom, right), Sonsedska Yuliia/SS (bottom, right), View Finder Nilsophon/SS (bottom, left); 103, Elena Shashkina/SS; 104, Africa Studio/SS, Saltodemata/SS (top, right), Iulius Costache/DRMS (middle, left), Anthro/DRMS (bottom, left), Artem Avetisyan/SS (bottom, left), Canadapanda/DRMS (bottom, right), Pukach/SS (bottom, right), Sebalos/DRMS (bottom, right); 106, Wabeno/DRMS (top, left), Anna Sedneva/DRMS (top, right), Pixfiction/SS (top, right), Shane Myers/DRMS (bottom, left), Dan Heighton/DRMS (bottom, right), Giuseppe_R/SS (bottom, right), Runrun2/SS (bottom, left); 107, Timbphotography/DRMS; 108, Xmee/SS (top), Kritchanut/DRMS (bottom), Suzanne Tucker/SS (bottom); 109, Michael Pettigrew/DRMS; 110, Joason Lester/DRMS (top, left), Photowitch/DRMS (bottom, left); 111, Maliutina Anna/SS, MidoSemsem/SS (middle); 112, Melanie F/DRMS; 114, Astra490/DRMS (top, left), Peter Zijlstra/SS (top, left), Aleksander Gligoric/DRMS (top, right), Jonathan Ross/Drms (bottom, left), Artiomp/SS (bottom, right), Flynt/DRMS (bottom, right), Goncharov2006/DRMS (bottom, right); 115, Martin Voeller/SS; 116,Fotoluminate LLC/SS (top), Jasmina Putnik/DRMS (top), Martin Bergsma/SS (top), Robin Joyce/SS (top), True Touch Lifestyle/SS (top), Yevgniy11/SS (top), Kolpakova Daria/SS (bottom); 117, Chiangcheng97/DRMS; 118, Egg Design/SS (top, left), Stuartbur/DRMS (top, left), Aperture Ssound/SS (top, right), Niko Dola/SS (top, right), Ivanna Pavliuk/DRMS (bottom, left), Jasmina Buinac/SS (bottom, right); 119, Martin Prochazkacz/SS; 120, Vaclav Sebek/DRMS; 122, Koldunova Anna/DRMS (top, right),Maggie 1/SS (bottom, left), Haywiremedia/DRMS (bottom, right);123, Mark Lindsay/SS; 124, Ramon Carretero/DRMS, Gvictoria/DRMS (bottom); 125, Broker/DRMS (top, left), Kosarieva Olena/DRMS (top, right), ZCW/SS (top, right), Hekla/SS (bottom, left); 126, Kristina Truniak/SS (top), Cammeraydave/DRMS (bottom), Kim Reinick/SS (bottom), Maphke93/DRMS (bottom), Valentin Valkov/SS (bottom); 127, Ongushi/SS; 128, New Africa/SS, Og-vision/DRMS (bottom); 130, Fotana/SS (top), Richard Peterson/SS (top, right), Irina Pingina/SS (bottom); 131, Pongchart B/SS; 132, Jithinraphy/SS (top, left), Mirelle/SS (bottom, left); 133, Karen Crewe/SS; 134, Nejron Photo/SS; 136, Red Confidential/SS (top, left), Logo Boom/SS (top, right), Draghicich/DRMS (bottom, left), Picha/Getty (bottom, left); 137, Andrey Armyagov/DRMS; 138, Magnus Binnerstam/DRMS; 139, Rudmer Zwerver/DRMS (top, right), Tatiana Popova/SS (top, right), Christian Delbert/DRMS (bottom), Denisa Prouzova/DRMS (bottom), Shane Myers Photography/SS (bottom), Pixelrobot/DRMS (bottom, right); 140, Adam Drobiec/DRMS (top, right), Blue Boeing/SS (bottom, left), Jiri Trubac/DRMS (bottom, left), Paul Binet/DRMS (bottom, left), Radhoose/DRMS (bottom, right); 141, Wonderly Imaging/SS, Michael Ledray/DRMS (left), Ruth Black/DRMS (left), Thomas Perkins/DRMS (left); 142, Kseniya Abramova/DRMS; 144, Par Edlund/DRMS (top), Elena Elisseeva/DRMS (bottom), Isselee/DRMS

(bottom), Rimglow/DRMS (bottom); 145, Vladimir Wrangel/SS; 146, Slowmotiongli/SS; 147, Chernetskaya/DRMS (top, left), Serg78/SS (top, right), Valentina_S/SS (bottom, right), Lukas Gojda/SS (bottom, right), New Africa/SS (bottom, left); 148, Javarman/DRMS; 150, Pavlina Trauskeova/SS (top, left), Lightkeeper/DRMS (top, right), Sergey Novikov/SS (bottom, left), Kiristopherk_SS (bottom, right); 151, Yxian076/DRMS; 152, Halbrindley/DRMS; 154, Docstockmedia/SS (top), Hans Slegers/SS (top), Jiang Hongyan/SS (top), Mega Pixel/SS (top), Ndanko/SS (top), Ekaterina Karpacheva/SS (bottom); 155, Linas T/SS; 156, Skynetphoto/DRMS (top); 156, Lucigerma/SS (bottom); 157, Kelly Ermis/DRMS; 158, Mikhail Blajenov/DRMS; 160, Sonsedska Yuliia/SS; 162, Fruii/DRMS (top, left), Elmiraot/SS (top, right), Andrew Anita/SS (bottom, left); 163, Kwanchaichaiudom/DRMS; 164, Dmytro Tolokonov/DRMS; 166, Chrisbrignell/SS (top), Gertan/SS (top), Milatiger/SS (bottom); 167, Mariia Loginovskaia/DRMS; 168, Kq333/SS, Andrey Stratilatov/SS (top), Maceofoto/SS (left), Mr. Yanukit/SS (middle, left), Oleksandrum/SS (right); 169, Pixelrobot/DRMS (middle, left), Alexander Raths/SS (middle, right), Danny E Hooks/SS (middle, right), Supertrooper/DRMS (middle, top), Dmytro Varavin/DRMS (bottom, left), Evgeny Karandaev/SS (bottom, left), Michael Flippo/DRMS (bottom, right); 170, Rejean Bedard/DRMS; 171, Carrie Fereday/SS (top, left), CapturePB/SS (bottom, left), K-Smile Love/SS (bottom, right), Ruslanchik/DRMS (bottom, left); 172, Chris Brignell/SS (top, left), Picure-Pets/SS (top, left), Dudarev Mikhail/SS (bottom, left), Eva Blanco/SS (top, right), Kuznetsov Alexey/SS (bottom, right), Yevgeniy11/SS (bottom, left); 173, Robert Bayer/DRMS; 174, Tatiana Popova/SS; 176, Isselee/DRMS (top, right), Pixel Embargo/SS (top, right), Sergii Kolesnyk/DRMS (top, right), FamVeld/SS (bottom, left); 177, Otsphoto/DRMS; 178, Dezy/SS, 179, Mark Herreid/DRMS (right), 180, Stockphoto Mania/SS; 181, Alle/SS (top, right), Ksegev/DRMS (right), Oleg Dudko/DRMS (right), Vnlit/SS (bottom, right), Anna Lohachova/SS (left), Pixelrobot/DRMS (bottom, right); 182, Photomaster/SS (top, left), Alexey Malashkevich/SS (top, right), Anphotos/DRMS (top, right), Alexander Potapov/DRMS (bottom, right), Kmitu/DRMS (bottom, right); 183, Riaan van-den Berg/SS; 184, Christopher Wood/DRMS (top, left), Martin Bergsma/DRMS (top, left), Przemyslaw Skibinski/SS (bottom, left); 185, DMV Photos/SS, 186, Photogerson/SS, FeelfFree/SS (bottom, left), Makkuro GL/SS (bottom, left), 187, Lebedinski/DRMS (bottom, left), Apolobay/DRMS (bottom, right), Ramona Smiers/DRMS (bottom, right), Margoe Edwards/SS (bottom); 188, Alex Hubenov/SS (left), Madlen/SS (left), Albert Beukhof/SS (right), Eric Isselee/SS (right), Hpphoto/DRMS (right), Stuartbur/DRMS (right), Veronika Surotseva/SS (right); 189, Steve Byland/DRMS; 190, Kuritafsheen/DRMS (bottom, left); 192, Photomaster/SS (top, left), Yellow Cat/SS (top, left), Pixelrobot/DRMS (top, right), PixieMe/SS (bottom, left), Broukoid/DRMS (bottom, right), Drawkman/SS (bottom, right); 193, Ondrej Prosicky/DRMS (bottom, left); 194, Fer Gregory/SS, Olgagillmeister/DRMS (bottom, left); 195, Eric Isselee/SS (left), Eric Isselee/SS (middle), Eric Isselee/SS (right), Natasha Zakharova/SS (bottom, left); 196, Masarik/SS (top, left), Vilmos Varga/DRMS (top, right), Sittichai Karimpard/DRMS (top, right), Eddie Dean/SS (bottom, left), Alfikih Rahmadani/SS (bottom, right); 197, Hakat/SS; 198, Olavs/SS (top), Nino Sayompoo/SS (middle), Ton Bangkeaw/SS (middle), Arctic Ice/SS (left); 199, TashaBubo/SS; 200, Leigh Prather/SS; Antonio Truzzi/SS (top, right), Albert Ziganshin/SS (middle), Buch/DRMS (right), Svetlana Foote/SS (bottom, left); 202, Dangdumrong/SS.

Since 1888, the National Geographic Society has funded more than 14,000 research, conservation, education, and storytelling projects around the world. National Geographic Partners distributes a portion of the funds it receives from your purchase to National Geographic Society to support programs including the conservation of animals and their habitats. To learn more, visit natgeo.com/info.

For more information, visit nationalgeographic .com, call 1-877-873-6846, or write to the following address:

National Geographic Partners, LLC
1145 17th Street N.W.
Washington, DC 20036-4688 U.S.A.

For librarians and teachers: nationalgeographic .com/books/librarians-and-educators

More for kids from National Geographic: natgeokids.com

National Geographic Kids magazine inspires children to explore their world with fun yet educational articles on animals, science, nature, and more. Using fresh storytelling and amazing photography, *Nat Geo Kids* shows kids ages 6 to 14 the fascinating truth about the world—and why they should care. **natgeo.com/subscribe**

For rights or permissions inquiries, please contact National Geographic Books Subsidiary Rights: bookrights@natgeo.com

Editorial, Design, and Production by Plan B Book Packagers

Trade paperback ISBN: 978-1-4263-7352-7
Reinforced library binding ISBN: 978-1-4263-7507-1

Printed in South Korea
22/SPSK/1